Flowers & Hearts & GARLANDS

QUILT

Liz Jones

Appliqué Masterpiece Series

American Quilter's Society
P. O. Box 3290 • Paducah, KY 42002-3290
www.AmericanQuilter.com

Located in Paducah, Kentucky, the American Quilter's Society (AQS) is dedicated to promoting the accomplishments of today's quilters. Through its publications and events, AQS strives to honor today's quiltmakers and their work and to inspire future creativity and innovation in quiltmaking.

EXECUTIVE BOOK EDITOR: ANDI MILAM REYNOLDS
COPY EDITOR: JACKIE FROEHLICH
GRAPHIC DESIGN: ELAINE WILSON
ILLUSTRATIONS: LYNDA SMITH
COVER DESIGN: MICHAEL BUCKINGHAM
HOW-TO PHOTOGRAPHY: LIZ JONES
QUILT PHOTOGRAPHY: CHARLES R. LYNCH

Additional copies of this book may be ordered from the American Quilter's Society, PO Box 3290, Paducah, KY 42002-3290, or online at www.AmericanQuilter.com.

Text © 2011, Author, Liz Jones
Artwork © 2011, American Quilter's Society

LIBRARY OF CONGRESS CATALOGING-IN-PUBLICATION DATA
Jones, Liz, 1946 May 2-
   Flowers, hearts, and garlands quilt / by Liz Jones.
      p. cm.
   Includes bibliographical references.
   ISBN 978-1-57432-648-2
   1. Machine appliqué. 2. Quilting. I. Title.
   TT779.J72 2011
   746.44'5--dc22
                              2011002933

TITLE PAGE: HEARTS AND GARLANDS, detail. Full quilt on page 6.

RIGHT: LOTUS, detail. Full quilt on page 8.

Dedication

||||||||||||||||||||||||||||||||||||||||||||||||||||||||||||||||||||||||||||||

To my three sons, Tony, Phil, and Rob

Acknowledgments

My thanks go to Carol Davies, Gill Hollingsworth, and all my other chums in Leominster Quilters who, with great patience, have let me bounce ideas off them; and to family and friends who have offered know-how and help when needed.

A big thank you to George Bromage for helping me with his invaluable computer skills.

Thanks to Claire Tinsley from Hannah's Room for fabric information.

I am indebted to Andi Reynolds at AQS for fielding all my questions and for inspiring confidence when it was needed.

Above all, thank you to Peter, my husband, for his constant encouragement, and for creating the time and space for this book to be written. He has uncomplainingly put up with an awful lot. Thanks Jonesy.

Contents

HEARTS AND GARLANDS, 76" x 76", made by the author

Introduction

Welcome to the wonderful world of machine appliqué!

HEARTS AND GARLANDS, page 6, came into being after I had been working on various appliqué techniques, searching for a way to liberate the creative process while maintaining quality control. That is, I needed to be able to appliqué any shape I wanted and to guarantee perfect placement at all times.

The method I've come up with fulfills both these criteria and at the same time has speeded up the process of my quiltmaking. I was so excited when I made the first quilt this way! LOTUS, page 8, was my "training ground."

I felt so free as I basted the fabrics into place by simply following the lines that I had drawn on the stabilizer paper (Fig. I–1).

The cutting out of the fabric was also a revelation as I had no fiddly little bits of fabric—just the finished shape in place when I had cut around the basting on the front (Fig. I–2). I had found my magic formula!

The shapes in LOTUS are quite big, but as I moved on to the satin-stitching stage, I realized that the lines, curves, angles, and points require just the same treatment whatever the size of a shape. This theory had to be tested out!

FIG. I–1. Free-motion machine basting

FIG I–2. Trimming around basting stitches on the front

LOTUS, 64" x 64", made by the author

Flowers, Hearts & GARLANDS QUILT ❀ LIZ JONES

OH TO BE IN NEW ENGLAND, 65" x 65", made by the author

The next quilt I tried the technique on was OH TO BE IN NEW ENGLAND, detail left, full quilt page 9, which has very small leaf shapes and lots of sharp points. The leaves had to be accurately placed for this design to work. For each tree, I used a fat quarter of variegated batik for the trunk and branches, and another for the leaves. (The fabric variation gives the impression of many different fabrics having been used, a useful tip to note.)

I free-motion basted the leaf shapes through the stabilizer paper, then cut around the basting of each leaf on the front. Yes, the points were tricky to start with, but I soon got the hang of what to do. All will be revealed in the following pages.

When I realized the liberating possibilities at my fingertips, inspiration from all sorts of sources started to flow. Eventually I knew I had enough ideas to create an album-style quilt; HEARTS AND GARLANDS is the result. As I worked I tried to treat each block as if it were a precious jewel, able to stand alone on its own strength, and to give it my very best. I couldn't wait to get up in the mornings to get sewing when I was making it!

If making the whole quilt seems too big a project for you, why not choose your four favorite blocks and make a wall quilt, or choose nine and make a lap quilt? A single block could be sized larger to make a lovely cushion, or a panel for a tote bag, or a single block wallhanging.

Having learned this machine-appliqué method and realizing that technique is no longer a barrier, why not have a go at designing your own piece? Anything is possible—set your imagination free and have fun!

Now read on and discover just how exciting machine appliqué can be…..

Part 1 *Equipment & Fabric Requirements*

EQUIPMENT AND SUPPLIES

Sewing Machine

- ❀ An electric sewing machine with a zigzag stitch
- ❀ A swing-stitch needle plate (also called a zigzag or general purpose or wide-hole throat plate)
- ❀ Feed dogs that can be lowered
- ❀ It is very useful to have a needle-down setting on the machine and a presser foot knee lift. These are not essential but they do make life easier.
- ❀ Open-toe darning foot or its equivalent (Fig. 1–1)
- ❀ Open-toe embroidery foot or its equivalent (Fig. 1–2)

Scissors

- ❀ Small, curved-bladed scissors for trimming threads
- ❀ A small pair of sharp scissors for trimming fabric away from the appliqué shapes
- ❀ A pair of large sewing scissors

Tweezers with Pointed Ends

Cutting Supplies

- ❀ Rotary cutting mat
- ❀ Rotary cutter
- ❀ 24" x 6" rotary cutting ruler and another 12½" x 12½" or larger

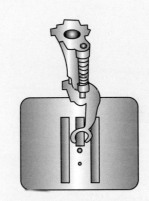

FIG. 1–1. Open-toe darning foot with straight-stitch needle plate and feed dogs dropped

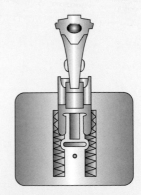

FIG. 1–2. Open-toe embroidery foot with swing needle plate and feed dogs raised

Marking Pen
- Black waterproof Pigma® Micron® pen #01 or #03

Light Box or a Strong Light Source

Tear-Away Lightweight Paper Stabilizer
- 12 packs 1 yard x 90 cm (36") or 12 yards from a 90cm (36") wide roll

Pressing Materials
- Iron and ironing board
- Spray starch
- Protective cloth for ironing board

Photocopier Access to make pattern enlargements

Quilting Tracing Paper
- One 12" wide roll (20 yards)

Temporary Spray Adhesive

FABRIC YARDAGE (40" WIDE FABRIC)

Background and Binding Fabric
- 11 yards

Appliqué fabrics: I relied heavily on my fabric stash when I made HEARTS AND GARLANDS, so it is not possible to give precise yardage for the appliqué. The following list is a generous approximation of quantities and colors for someone who has no fabrics before starting to make the quilt. I love the richness of Bali batik fabrics, and the endless variations of the Bali Hand-Dyed Watercolors from Hoffman Fabrics. Their colors are vibrant and the weave is firm and not prone to fray easily.

Number of fat quarters needed: You will need half yards if you feel you will use more of a particular color.

- ❁ 1 off-white
- ❁ 3 different reds
- ❁ 4 " light browns/beiges
- ❁ 8 " yellows
- ❁ 8 " blues/turquoises
- ❁ 12 " pinks/peaches
- ❁ 12 " purples/mauves
- ❁ 12 " greens
- ❁ ¼ yard of multicolored batik fabric for the 24 border hearts
- ❁ And any other fabrics that you fall in love with!

Piping

- ❁ ½ yard of contrast fabric
- ❁ 9 yards of ½" cord

Backing

- ❁ 6 yards. I used a Moda Marble here as well as for the background fabric, where the joins between the blocks blend together well and are hardly visible.

Batting

- ❁ Queen size batt (or 84" x 84")

Lightweight Fusible Web

- ❁ ¼ yard to appliqué the small hearts onto the border after the top is pieced

Needles

- ❁ 80/12 Schmetz Microtex Sharp machine needles for the basting and the satin stitching
- ❁ 60/8 Schmetz Microtex Sharp machine needles for the quilting

Threads

Bobbin Thread

- ❁ A fine dark neutral or black polyester bobbin thread is my personal choice unless you are working with a light background fabric.

Basting Thread

- ❁ This will never show in your work, so I suggest something similar to the bobbin thread, 50 wt. or 60 wt.

Satin Stitch Thread

- ❁ I have used 40 wt. rayon thread of any brand. Make your choice according to the types of colors you have selected for your appliqué fabrics. Think in terms of lights, mediums, and darks for each of your color groups.

Quilting Thread

- ❁ I used 100 wt. silk thread, but any fine quilting thread would do. Fine thread is less likely to cause surface distortion in a heavily quilted piece such as this.

Contrast piping, detail

PART 2
Stitching Techniques

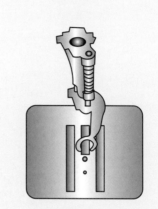

FIG. 2–1. Open-toe darning foot with straight-stitch needle plate and feed dogs dropped

FREE-MOTION STITCHING IN GENERAL

For basting the appliqué and for free-motion quilting, you will need:

- a darning/quilting/walking foot
- a straight-stitch needle (or throat) plate, but if you only have the swing-stitch needle plate it will be fine
- *dropped* feed dogs, as if for darning (Fig. 2–1)
- dark/neutral 60 wt. thread top and bottom

I set the stitch length to zero (0) because there is no point in the feed dogs being dropped out of commission and leaving them churning away under the needle plate. The less they work the less wear on the machine, and the machine will be quieter as you work. As I sew I am constantly aware of the sound of the machine—both the motor and the mechanics—and I listen to what they are saying. A happy purring sound is the ideal, so any change from that and I like to know why.

Because the feed dogs are down, and, as they are the stitch length regulators during normal sewing, obviously you are now in total control of the length of stitch you make as you baste or free-motion quilt. Wonderful liberation! You are free to sew in any direction you want, with any size stitch you want and at whatever speed you want. (Warning, this method of sewing can become addictive!)

Flowers, Hearts & GARLANDS QUILT ❀ LIZ JONES

FREE-MOTION APPLIQUÉ BASTING

Set up the machine as on page 14.

This line stitching (basting) that you will do over the block drawings on the paper stabilizer will remain in your work, under the satin stitching. It will not be removed and it will not show in the finished piece. I use any black or darkish neutral-colored 60 wt. thread in the bobbin and top of the machine for all the basting.

Before starting to sew, always bring the bobbin thread to the surface by holding the top thread and making one stitch and gently pulling up the bobbin thread with the top thread. This avoids tangled threads at the beginning of any sewing (Fig. 2–2).

I hold on to these two threads with your left hand as you start to sew. Keep the basting stitches quite small; you won't be removing them. There is no need to worry about securing the starts and finishes, as these stitches will be covered up later on.

FREE-MOTION QUILTING

A *helpful notion to remember is this:* Speed equals distance (stitch length) over time. Therefore, stitch length is the rate at which you make the needle go up and down multiplied by the rate at which your hands move the fabric under the needle. I find that bearing this in mind helps to keep my stitches more even in length.

Make yourself a test piece by drawing some curved lines and some closed shapes on spare paper stabilizer. Pin this to the back of a piece of scrap spray-starched fabric and practice your free-motion basting stitches. Don't worry about following any lines to begin with. Just get the feel of the stitching by moving the fabric under the needle in different directions. Then practice your line control over the drawn lines.

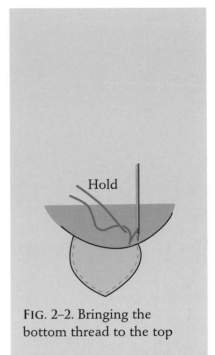

Hold

FIG. 2–2. Bringing the bottom thread to the top

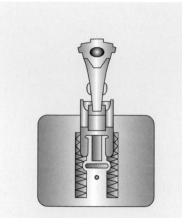

FIG. 2–3. Open-toe embroidery foot with swing needle plate and feed dogs raised

SATIN STITCHING

Make sure the needle (throat) plate on your sewing machine is the correct one for swing needle (zigzag) work, that is, the one with a slit in it, NOT the straight-stitch (round hole) needle plate. The wrong needle plate = instant broken needle!

I find the best sewing foot for satin stitch is the open-toe embroidery foot, as it allows a clear view of where you are going to be sewing. Feed dogs must be in the raised (normal) position (Fig. 2–3).

Set the machine to the needle-down position. If you don't have this function on your machine, remember to stop with the needle down in the work if you are still working on an edge and will be lifting the presser foot for a curve or a point. A machine with a (presser foot) knee lift is a great help, especially when sewing curves, because it leaves your hands free, but it can be done just as well by manually lifting the presser foot each time the fabric is turned.

Needles

I use Schmetz Microtex needles for everything. My machine and most of my threads and fabrics seem happy with them for straight stitch, free-motion stitching, and satin stitch. I use as small a needle as the thickness of thread will allow, usually a 70 or 80, but this is something you will have to test for yourself as fabrics, machines, and threads vary so much. Follow thread manufacturers' advice where it is available.

Stitch Length Setting

A *second* layer of paper stabilizer must be pinned over the first (drawing) layer of paper on the back of the fabric whenever satin stitch is being sewn. This is to prevent the satin stitch from pulling in the fabric and puckering the surface. Do this with your basting test piece and use it to test your satin stitch settings, working from the front of the work now.

Just as when basting, bring the bobbin thread to the top and hold the two threads as you begin stitching. Set your machine on zigzag stitch and test how long the stitch length must be to produce a rich, close satin stitch, being careful not to make it too dense or lumpy. You do not want to be able to see the fabric between the stitches. Once you have found the best stitch density for yourself, that stitch length setting should remain constant throughout the project.

Stitch Width Setting

The stitch width setting will vary according to the look you want to achieve; too narrow and the basting stitches will not be covered and the raw edges of the appliqué pieces will pull out and fray. Zigzag stitches that are too wide may result in a heavy look. Start with the width somewhere around 2mm. Then try narrower and wider until you are happy with the look.

Not all appliqué pieces will require the same width of satin stitch and sometimes it will be appropriate to vary the width of the stitches *as you are sewing* a shape, to add dimension and interest to the shape. Try out your ideas on your test piece and, for future reference, write on the fabric next to the sample stitching what you did and what settings you used.

Starts and Stops

I recommend reducing the stitch width when starting a whole shape (one not overlapped by another), for example, a complete circle or leaf (Fig. 2–4).

When you finish the satin stitch by overlapping the starting stitches you will be sure to cover the slightly narrower start stitches. To secure the finishing threads, either:

❀ Remove the work from the machine and secure the threads by pulling the top thread to the back of the work and tying the two threads securely together; or

❀ Secure the threads by reducing the stitch width to 0.5mm and sew in reverse for about ⅛". Trim the top thread at the surface of the work, remove the work from the machine, and trim the back thread to about 1" from the work.

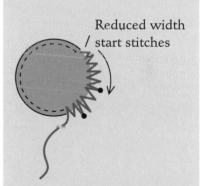

Reduced width start stitches

FIG. 2–4. Starting stitching a whole shape

Machine Tension Setting

I reduce the top tension on my machine in order to give a richness to the satin stitch by allowing the top thread to pass through and curve just a little around to the back of the fabric, rather than having the top and bottom threads lock at the surface of the fabric, which results in a flatter looking stitch. This is purely *my* choice, but it does have the advantage that the color of the bobbin can be the same for all the different top thread colors, as it is highly unlikely to ever show on the top. I use a fine black or neutral bobbin thread.

I must strongly recommend that you practice your stitching in order to produce the look *you* want. I spend a lot of time setting up the machine to sew just how I want for a particular project. I write all the settings down on the actual fabric sample so I will know just what's what at a later date. I also glue or tack bits of paper with information for myself onto the machine. Don't kid yourself that you will *remember* the settings—life's not like that!

The satin stitch on the appliqué in HEARTS AND GARLANDS was sewn in several 40 wt. rayon threads using many different brands. Rayon thread gives satin stitch a deep, rich luster, which I believe is a perfect enhancement to the intense, vibrant colors of the batik fabrics in many of the appliqué motifs. A softer effect would be achieved by using 50 wt. cotton thread.

Curves

As a general rule, work with the appliqué area to the left of the needle, sewing clockwise.

Remember, use *two* layers of paper stabilizer when sewing satin stitch.

Always stop with the needle in the *down* position on the *outside* of any curved line, irrespective of whether the outside of the curve is on the inside of the appliqué piece or on the outer edge. Figs. 2–5 through 2–8 on pages 19 and 20 show black dots indicating crucial needle-down pivot points.

Raise the presser foot and pivot your work so that the next stitch will keep the stitches at right angles to the sewing edge. As you start to sew, turn the work a little in the direction and shape of the curve, taking care not to distort the fabric.

Stop with the needle down before the angle of the stitches becomes too oblique to the sewing edge. This you will gauge by experience.

The distance you will be able to sew before stopping and turning again will also depend on the tightness of the curve; the tighter the curve, the more stops and turns you will need to do. You will soon find that you don't have to raise the presser foot all the way up every time, but just enough to be able to turn the work without obstruction.

By easing the fabric around under the presser foot, a wide arc curve is sometimes possible to sew in one continuous movement. Even then it is often better to sew in stages to avoid any fabric distortion.

Ideally, someone looking at your quilt should not be aware that the curve has been sewn in increments. If the curve looks rather angular in places, this is probably because you did not stop and turn the work often enough on that particular curve.

The wider the satin stitch is set on the machine, the more stops and turns will be required to keep the stitching looking effortlessly smooth. Sewn with care and patience, a wider stitch setting can look very beautiful and dramatic.

Corners and Points

Right angles and obtuse angles are treated the same way: Stop with the needle down on the outer edge of the point (A) (Fig. 2–5).

Turn the work, ready to stitch along the next side. Carefully overstitch the first few stitches on the corner; then continue the sewing (Fig. 2–6).

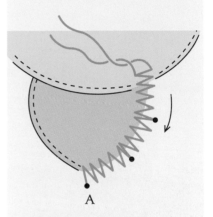

FIG. 2–5. Stop with needle down on the outside of the point.

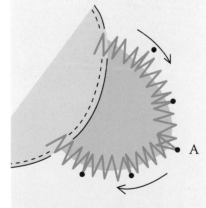

FIG. 2–6. Pivot the work around at A to sew in the direction of the next side.

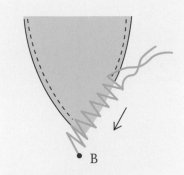

FIG. 2–7. Showing pivot point B

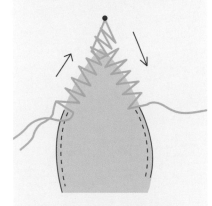

FIG. 2–8. Work turned on point with stitches pulled gently at an angle to keep the point sharp

Points or more acute angles are a little more tricky. As you approach the point you may want to try reducing the width of the satin stitch very slightly in order to make it a little more delicate.

You will need to gently but firmly slightly twist and pull your work while still sewing in the same direction. This will make the stitches sew at an oblique angle, making the point narrower and therefore more pointed.

Stop with the needle down just beyond the apex of the point (B) and pivot the work (Fig. 2–7).

Again, you will need to make the stitches sew at a bit of an angle to keep that point looking sharp as you sew away from it (Fig. 2–8).

These little pulls to achieve good corners and points will take a bit of practice, but when you get the hang of it I think you will be pleased with the results.

PART 3
Stitching the Appliqué

KEY TO DIAGRAMS

————	Drawn line (to stitch along)
- - - - -	Stitched line
\/\/\/\/\/	Satin stitch
Dark/pale	Front/back of fabrics
White	Tear-away paper stabilizer
-- --I	Pin

FIG. 3–1. Tudor Rose sample drawing

Trace the Tudor Rose block sample onto a piece of paper stabilizer (Fig. 3–1).

Spray starch a sample piece of background fabric a couple of times and lightly spray starch the appliqué fabric bits. Pin the *back* of the drawing to the *back* of the background fabric (Fig. 3–2).

FIG. 3–2. Pin back of drawing to back of fabric.

ORDER OF STITCHING

As a general rule, the order of stitching is as follows:

1 – Stems on the background fabric
2 – Appliqué the pieces farthest back first, building up to the top pieces
3 – Stems over the top of appliqué pieces

Basting is done from the paper stabilizer side, over the drawn lines.

Satin stitching is done from the front side of the fabric, following either the basted lines of stitching (stems) or the trimmed edges of the basted appliqué.

STEMS

Set the machine for free-motion stitching (see page 14).

Starts and stops do not need to be secured; it is fine to backtrack over stitching to avoid them. There is no need to worry about being too accurate because "tram lines" (track lines) won't show; these are only indicator lines and will be covered by satin stitches.

Starting at one end of the main stem, branch to the left and then back to the right, then back up the side stems.

Then continue to the end of the main stem. Keep the stitches shorter than a seam stitch length. Be sure to stitch over into the appliqué shapes that will overlap the stems (Fig. 3–3).

Remove the work from the machine and turn it to the right side. This now shows the stitched guide lines for the satin stitch stems.

Set the machine for satin stitching (see page 16).

You are now going to do satin stitching for a short time, *just on the stems,* so it is necessary to

FIG. 3–3. Stitched guidelines for stems

pin a second piece of paper stabilizer to the back of the work. Be sure the second layer of stabilizer covers all the stems to be sewn. It is not necessary to cover the whole of the back of the work as long as the areas to be sewn are covered.

Always use *two layers* of stabilizer when sewing any machine satin stitch, as this prevents the stitches from pulling up and puckering the work.

Satin stitching the stems has to be done out of order so that the appliqué can cover the stem starts and stops.

Working from the front of the work, start with the side stems first (Fig. 3–4). As all of these will be covered by either more satin stitching or an appliqué piece, there is no need to secure the starts or stops.

When you sew the main stem, start at an open end, that is, one that is not overlapped. Backstitch very narrow zigzag stitches about ¼" before the start of the stem, trim the two threads close to the surface, then sew forward with the zigzag setting for the stem, covering the backstitching. This will produce a sharp, neat and secure start (Fig. 3–5).

When all the stems are complete, carefully but firmly tear away the *plain* piece of paper stabilizer that was added for sewing the satin stitch stems. DO NOT REMOVE THE PAPER STABILIZER DRAWING. By leaving the drawing in place you will achieve correct placement of the appliqué pieces onto the stems.

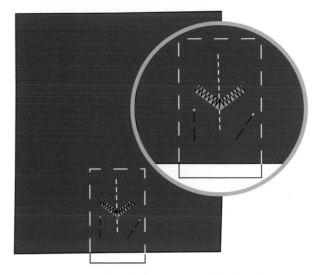

FIG. 3–4. Second piece of stabilizer pinned behind stem area. Side stems satin stitched.

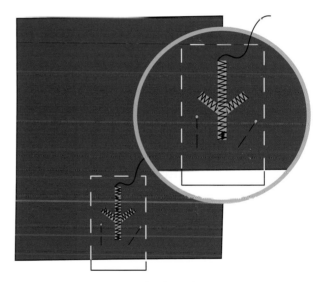

FIG. 3–5. Main stem satin stitched with a secure start at the bottom

FIG. 3–6. Tulips (D2), detail showing stems passing over appliqué pieces

FIG. 3–7. Iris (B2), detail showing stems passing over appliqué pieces

FIG. 3–8. Peach Blooms (D4), detail showing stems passing over appliqué pieces

Exception: Four blocks, Tulips (D2), Iris (B2), Peach Blooms (D4), and Basket Bouquet (B4), all have some stems that pass *over* some of the appliqué (Figs. 3–6 through 3–9).

Do the free-motion basting to indicate the position of the overlapping stems *after* the appliqué has been basted on. By studying these blocks when you come to do them, you will understand when to baste the stem lines and when to satin stitch them. These four blocks are best approached after you have completed some of the more straightforward blocks, especially Iris.

FIG. 3–9. Basket Bouquet (B4), detail showing stems passing over appliqué pieces

APPLIQUÉING THE PIECES

Basting

Set the machine for free-motion stitching (see page 14).

Layering of the appliqué fabrics involves working from the farthest-back pieces forward to the frontmost pieces.

Always baste from about ⅛" to ¼" into the overlapping area if the piece you are sewing is behind another shape. Mark these overlapping sewing lines onto your paper to follow as you sew until you are used to the technique.

In this example, Tudor Rose (A1), the outside small green leaves are the farthest back (Fig. 3–10).

Notes and reminders can be jotted onto the paper stabilizer, for example, dashes of felt tip on the areas to be basted in that particular color.

Pin the *back* of the green (leaf) fabric to the *front* of the background fabric. Be sure the fabric to be appliquéd is large enough to cover all the areas that you will be sewing. You can check this by holding the layered work up to a strong light or by laying the work over a light box. Sew around the two main and five small outer green leaves, including the overlapped areas.

When all of the first layer of leaves has been sewn, remove the work from the machine. Turn the piece over and with small sharp scissors trim about ¹⁄₁₆" from the stitching (Fig. 3–11).

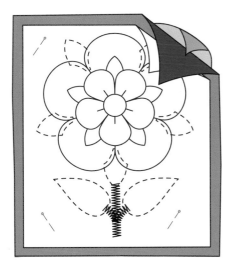

FIG. 3–10. Back of green fabric pinned to front of background fabric. Stem leaves and small leaves on outside edge of flower are basted.

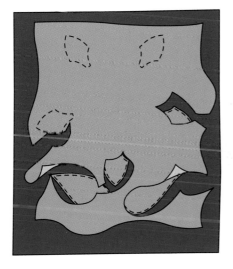

FIG. 3–11. Trimming around basted shapes on the right side of the piece

FIG. 3–12. Orange fabric pinned in place. Sewing lines showing where large petals go over the outside leaves and under the inside leaves and small petals.

FIG. 3–13. Trimming basted orange petals

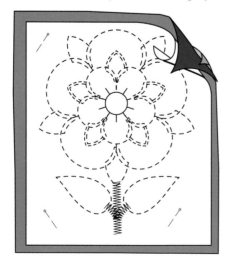

FIG. 3–14. Small green leaves basted showing extended stitching into small petals

I try to cut economically, as often a small piece of fabric is useful on another block later on. In this case the center of the green fabric should be large enough to cover the entire area of the inner leaves. *Warning: Be very careful not to snip into the background fabric when you are trimming the shapes. It is too easily done!*

Pin the *back* of the next layer of fabric, in this case the orange for the outer large petals, onto the *front* of the work. Check over your light source that the orange fabric is large enough to include the whole orange area. Mark the overlapped parts under the inner leaves and inner petals on your drawing (Fig. 3–12).

Then sew on the line of the extended shape and remove the work from the machine. Turn it over and carefully trim the orange fabric close to the stitches (Fig. 3–13).

Repeat the appliqué basting stitches on the next layer, the inner leaves, noting where you extend the stitch lines to create the overlaps (Fig. 3–14).

FIG. 3–15. Trimming small leaves

Remove the work from the machine, turn, and trim (Fig. 3–15, page 26).

The block is now ready for the small inner petals and the center. Repeat the above steps with the pale orange fabric (Figs. 3–16 and 3–17) and the yellow center of the flower (Fig. 3–18).

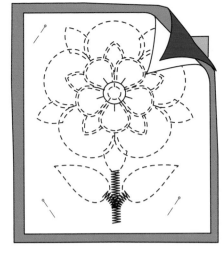

FIG. 3–16. Pale orange inner petals basted

FIG. 3–17. Inner petals trimmed

FIG. 3–18. Flower center basted and trimmed

Note: *Sometimes you will have a number of smaller pieces of a particular appliqué fabric left, none of which will be quite large enough to cover all areas of that color in one go. No problem. Just note which pieces are covered by one piece of fabric, by holding the work up to the light. Baste them, then pin other bits of fabric over the remaining pieces of the same color. You may have to do this two or three times for a particular color as you get further into making all the blocks for the whole quilt.*

FIG. 3–19. Heart Tree (E3), detail showing use of multicolored variegated fabric

FIG. 3–20. Carnations (E1), detail showing variegated thread used with variegated fabric

FIG. 3–21. Holly and Ivy (B5), detail showing how changing the satin stitch color can alter the look of a fabric—in this case the holly leaves

Using variegated batiks can make a block or a flower look as though it has been constructed out of many different fabrics. For example, in Heart Tree (E3) I used one fabric for the trunk and branches, then one fabric for the leaves. Carnations (E1) shows the effect of variegated thread used with variegated fabric. In Holly and Ivy (B5), the holly leaves are one fabric, but by having changed the color of the satin stitch threads, each leaf looks different (Figs. 3–19 through 3–21).

I'm always excited when anticipating the serendipitous results that these fabrics can create. It is good not to try to be in total control all the time and to allow the magic of the fabrics to surprise us. Remember: There is no right or wrong; if *you* like it, go for it!

Satin Stitching the Edges

Set the machine for satin stitching (see page 16).

Reminder: Before the appliqué edges are satin stitched, a second piece of paper stabilizer must be pinned over the drawn piece on the back of the work.

Working from the front of the piece, the order of satin stitching is, in principle, the same as that of free-motion basting. So, again, you will start with the farthest back pieces and any free-standing pieces (not overlapped/overlapping). *You will have to change the top thread each time the color of the appliqué changes.*

In each block the farthest back pieces are the small outer green leaves. As the starts and stops are going to be sewn over by the next layer of satin stitch, there is no need to secure them. This applies to all the satin stitching in the Tudor Rose (A1) sample except for the flower center and the two stem leaves, as they are not overlapped or overlapping any other piece. Continue sewing around each layer in order (Fig. 3–22).

Note: *There is an exception to the order of stitching. When the satin stitch doesn't go over any other shape you can save time by keeping the green thread in the machine and sew the inner leaves before the outer orange petals are sewn.*

When all of the appliqué has been satin stitched, the two layers of paper can be removed. It is better to tear away one layer at a time to minimize the stress on the stitches. Pointed tweezers are useful for removing the smaller pieces of paper (Fig. 3–23).

Alternate approach: The flowers in Wisteria (C1) were satin-stitch embroidered but it would be perfectly possible to appliqué the small shapes of the flowers (Fig. 3–24).

To mark the position of the flowers on the block for embroidery, baste the shapes through on to the front of the background as if marking a stem (see page 22). To embroider the flowers, use the satin stitch setting and turn the zigzag width wider or narrower as you sew to create the flowers. This will need a little practice. It is the same method I used to embroider the petal shapes on the Rose Square (A4) (Fig. 3–25, page 30).

Now you have all the techniques at your fingertips to be able to start making the blocks.

FIG. 3–22. Second piece of stabilizer pinned in place. Drawing shows order of satin stitch to cover starts and stops where possible.

FIG. 3–23. Removing paper stabilizer

FIG. 3–24. Wisteria (C1), detail of embroidered flowers. These could be appliquéd just as well.

FIG. 3–25. Rose Square (A4), detail showing satin stitching of the petals

BLOCK PREPARATION AND CUTTING PLAN

Note: *It is important to cut the background blocks a generous size for two reasons. First, even though stabilizer is used for all the appliqué, I find that there is still a considerable reduction in the size of the background fabric blocks due to the sheer amount of stitching on them; and second, because the block is turned and handled so much during the sewing, a greater trimming allowance is needed in case the edges of the blocks become scruffy and out of shape.*

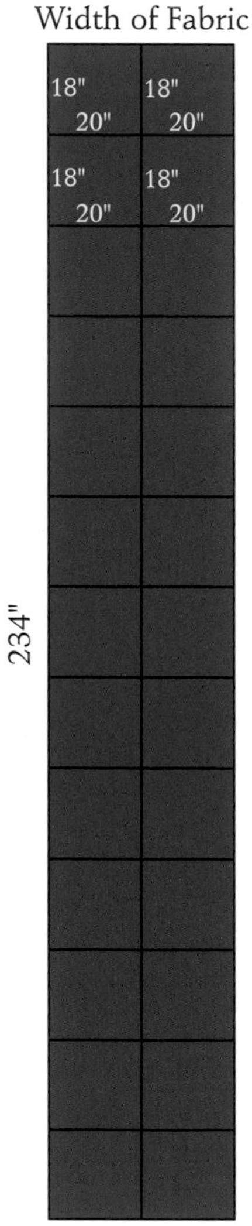

FIG. 3–26. Cutting layout for the 25 center blocks background

FIG. 3–27. Cutting layout for the 28 border blocks background

Note: The 11 yards of background fabric called for assumes very accurate cutting precisely according to these diagrams. You will have less than 3" of fabric remaining, so you may choose to increase the yardage for insurance.

25 Center Blocks

Fig. 3–26 shows the layout that will make 18" x 20" backgrounds for the center blocks, which finish 12½" x 12½".

28 Border Blocks (24 side blocks and 4 corner blocks)

Fig. 3–27 shows the layout that will make background blocks each 13" x 13". These wil finish approximately 10½" x 10½".

Binding

Nine 3¼" x 40" wide strips cut from the width of the fabric (Fig. 3–28, page 31). Note: The binding is ½" finished.

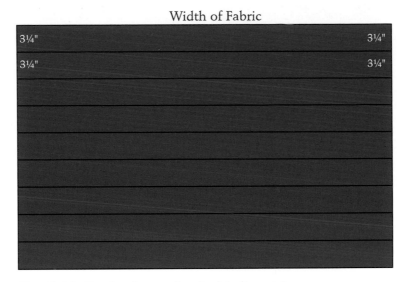

Width of Fabric

3¼"   3¼"

3¼"   3¼"

FIG. 3–28. Cutting layout for the binding strips.

Piping Fabric

8" x 2" strips cut from the width of the fabric

Tear-Away Stabilizer

For the 25 center blocks cut 50 squares 12" x12" (2 for each block). You can cut 9 squares from 1 yard of 36" wide stabilizer

For the 28 border blocks cut 56 pieces 9" x 10" (2 for each block). You can cut 12 pieces this size from 1 yard of 36" wide stabilizer.

Mark the centers of the 25 center block pieces and 28 border block pieces.

PREPARING THE APPLIQUÉ DRAWINGS

Note: *Remember that the finished image on the right side of your work will be the reverse of what you draw on the paper stabilizer. A symmetrical image is not affected.*

Use a waterproof pen to avoid the risk of pencil or ink transferring from your hands to your work.

Preparing the Center Blocks

Using a scanner or photocopier enlarge the 25 center block drawings by 200%.

Trace each full size drawing onto a 12" square of paper stabilizer. Align the center of the stabilizer with the center of each drawing.

Matching all centers, pin the back of the drawing to the back of the fat quarter of starched background fabric. You may prefer to hand tack the paper stabilizer to the fabric around the outer edge.

This paper stabilizer with the drawing will not be removed until the whole block is completed.

Matching the centers is important as it ensures that there will be enough fabric around the edges to trim the blocks accurately when they have been sewn, prior to piecing them together.

Note: *Iris (B2) will need 2 drawings—one of just the leaves (a) and one of the leaves and the flowers (b). The leaves must be completed with all their satin stitching before the Iris flowers are appliquéd over the top of them. Align the second drawing over the first drawing on the back of the block to ensure the correct position of the flowers.*

Preparing the Border Blocks

The border blocks are already at full size. Trace each one onto a 9" x 10" piece of paper stabilizer. Align the center of the stabilizer with the center of each drawing.

Matching all centers, pin the back of the drawing to the back of the 13" x 13" piece of starched background fabric.

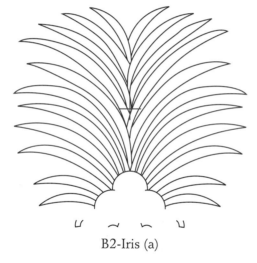

B2-Iris (a)

B2-Iris (b)

PART 4

Quilt Top Construction

TRIMMING AND JOINING BLOCKS

When all the paper stabilizer bits have been removed from the back of the blocks, *steam* press each block from the back. Gently pull and ease any distortion that may have occurred during the sewing. Lightly spray starch from the back and *dry* iron the blocks really flat.

The following cutting measurements include the ¼" seam allowance.

Trimming the Center Blocks

Keeping the center of the appliqué at the center of the squares, trim the blocks to 12½" x 12½".

Trimming the 24 Border Blocks

Referring to Fig. 4–1, keep the appliqué centered between the left and right sides. Trim each block 10½" wide. Trim across the block, leaving a 2¼" allowance between the tops of the appliquéd garland ends and cutting line. *Do not trim the outer edges of the blocks at this stage (this will be done after the quilting is finished).*

Trimming the Corner Blocks

Referring to Fig. 4–2, page 34, measure 6½" from the center of the appliqué along the diagonal in the direction of the open end of the design (point A). Lay the 45-degree line of your square ruler along the diagonal AD with the corner at A. By trimming along AB and AC, the block will be sized correctly for piecing. *Do not trim the two outer edges at this stage.*

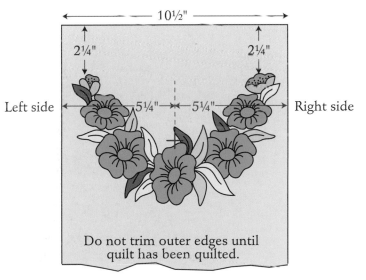

FIG. 4–1. Measurements for cutting the 24 side border blocks

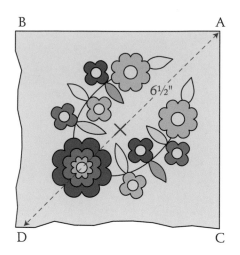

FIG. 4–2. Measurements for cutting the 4 corner border blocks

ASSEMBLING THE QUILT TOP

A ¼" seam allowance is used in constructing the quilt top.

Unless you have chosen another layout, refer to the photograph of HEARTS AND GARLANDS on page 6 or the Appliqué Block Layout Diagram on page 41 for the block placement.

Join the center blocks into 5 strips of 5 blocks. Press the seams open (Fig. 4–3).

Join the five strips. Press the seams open.

To join the border blocks, refer to Fig. 4–4.

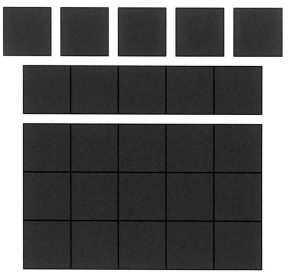

FIG. 4–3. Order for joining the 25 center blocks

FIG. 4–4. Order for joining the border blocks

Join the 6 side blocks together for 2 sides. Press the seams open. Join these strips to the top and bottom of the center blocks. Note that the block seams do not match. Press the seams open.

Join the remaining 2 sides' blocks together, adding a corner block to each end of each side. Press the seams open. Join these two borders to the quilt top and press the seams open. Again, block seams do not match.

ADDING THE SMALL APPLIQUÉ HEARTS

Trace 24 of the small open heart pattern (Fig. 4–5 is an actual-size template) onto the fusible web. Iron it to the back of the heart fabric and cut out. Iron each heart into position, as shown on the photograph of HEARTS AND GARLANDS on page 6.

Satin stitch around the inside and the outside of each heart. When all hearts are complete, press the whole top again.

Actual size

FIG. 4–5. Small open heart appliqué pattern

BACKING

Divide the 6 yards of backing fabric into 2 lengths of 3 yards. With right sides together, join the two pieces. Press the seam open.

BATTING

Lay the batting out for about a week before layering the quilt to allow any creases to ease out and so it can recover its loft and shape.

I prefer wool batting as it is light, retains its loft, is not too bulky, and machine quilts beautifully. A good brand of polyester batting would be fine. I do not recommend cotton in this instance as it would be rather stiff with a quilt so heavily machine appliquéd.

Layering and Basting

Layer the backing, batting, and quilt top and baste in your usual way. My choice for preparing for machine quilting is to use curved basting safety pins. I have discovered that everyone has their own preference as to which is the best method for basting, and they are firmly dedicated to their way. I will not attempt to convert anyone at this point!

Trim excess backing and batting to about 2" more than the top fabric, unless you're sending your top to a longarm quilter; check with her or him about the preferred trim size. If you are doing the quilting yourself by hand or domestic machine, fold about 1½" of the backing over to the front. Tack in place to make a neat temporary working edge.

PART 5
Quilting & Finishing

Prepare the machine as for free-motion quilting (see page 15).

Make some quilting test pieces using the same fabrics as the top, batting, and backing.

Thread the machine with quilting thread (I used 100 wt. silk threads) and the appropriate needle. I always use a new needle before starting to quilt, and with a quilt this size (76" x 76"), I replace it at least once during the quilting. When quilting I wear cotton quilting gloves that have lots of little grippy blobs on the fingers, thumbs, and palms. I "puddle" the area of the quilt that I am sewing; I am not a "folder" or a "roller." Do as you please; this is just the way that works for me.

Draw some leaves, flowers, and stems on the top of the test piece and practice your free-motion quilting going around the shapes. Practice some vermicelli quilting. Evenness of stitching is what you are aiming for but don't worry too much about attaining perfection—it doesn't exist!

Start quilting by bringing the bottom thread up as usual, then stitch 6–8 stitches very, very close to each other. Then gradually over about ½", lengthen the stitches to the desired length and off you go.

Finish a run of quilting by sewing as at the beginning with 6–8 very close stitches. Trim the top thread at the surface. Trim the bottom thread by pulling the work a little from the needle area, peeping and feeling under the quilt and trimming the bobbin thread close to the under surface with small curved scissors; no need to remove the quilt from the machine every time.

Wherever possible, backtrack along previous quilting lines to avoid unnecessary starts and stops.

ORDER OF QUILTING

Starting from the center block and working out, quilt about ¹⁄₁₆" away from the edges of all the appliqué.

Where the shapes overlap, change the thread to a more appropriate color if the pieces are lighter, and work inside the separate flowers and leaves (Figs. 5–1 and 5–2).

The garlands are echo-quilted another ⅛" from the first quilting around the appliqué, as are the small appliquéd hearts joining the garlands (Fig. 5–3).

PREPARING THE QUILTING PATTERNS

Refer to Fig. 5–4 on page 38 for the key to quilting pattern placements.

Enlarge quilting patterns #1 to #16 by 200 percent. Pattern numbers 17 to 42 are full size. Number each design and indicate the top of the design (which way is up).

Trace each design and its number and orientation 1 time onto a piece of Golden Threads Quilting Paper using a waterproof pen such as Pigma Micron 01. Exceptions: Trace pattern #41 (24) times and pattern #42 (28) times.

As you prepare to sew a quilting pattern, lightly spray the back of the drawn tissue with 505® Spray and Fix Temporary Adhesive and let it dry completely (about a minute). Press into place according to the key, and pin the four corners.

FIG. 5–1. Yellow Garland, detail showing the quilting in the yellow flowers

FIG. 5–2. Basket Bouquet (B4), detail showing changes of quilting thread color within the flowers and leaves

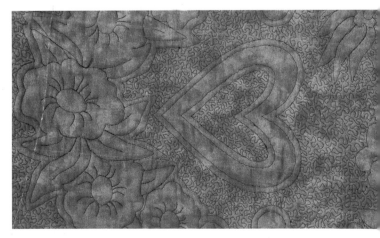

FIG. 5–3. Back of quilt showing echo quilting around the garlands and heart motifs

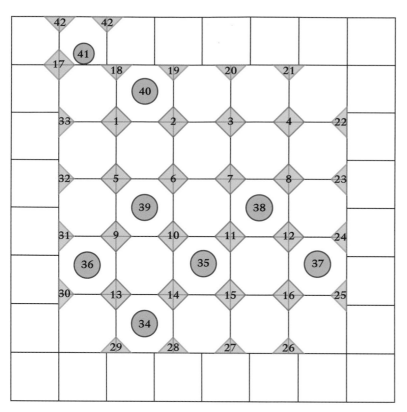

FIG. 5–4. Key to quilting design placement

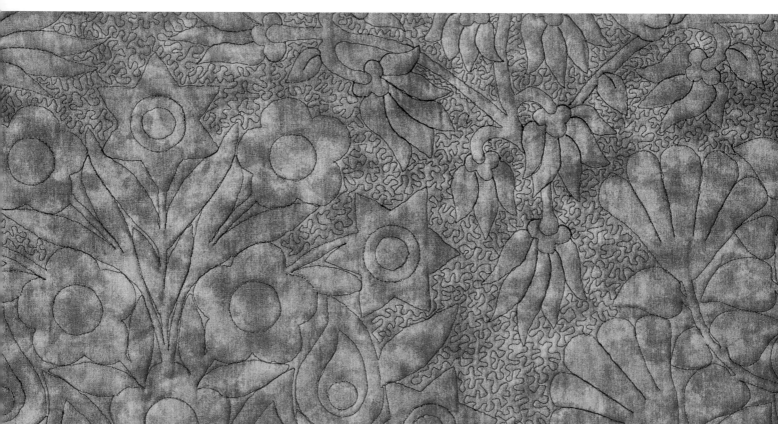

FIG. 5–5. Back of quilt detail showing quilting around quilting and appliqué motifs and vermicelli quilting

Free-motion quilt through the paper, backtracking when necessary. Tear away the tracing paper. Repeat for all 40 designs and for the 24 large hearts and circles and 28 small heart shapes. Free-motion vermicelli quilt between all the quilted shapes, taking the vermicelli out to at least 2" beyond the curved bottoms of the garlands. Fig. 5–3, page 37 and Fig. 5–5, page 38 show the back of the quilt with quilting lines and placement examples.

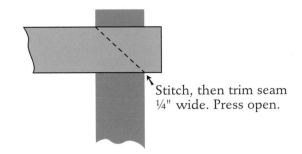

Stitch, then trim seam ¼" wide. Press open.

FIG. 5–6. Method of joining binding strips and piping strips

PIPING

Join 2 strips together for each side of the quilt to create 4 pieces (Fig. 5–6).

Fold each piece in half lengthwise, right-side out, with the piping cord tucked tightly into the fold. Using a zipper foot, stitch as close as possible to the covered piping (Fig. 5–7).

Trim to a ½" seam allowance. Note that the binding will be ½" wide, not the more usual ¼".

Trim one side of the quilt 1½" from the base of the garland appliqués (Fig. 5–8).

With a quilt pencil mark the cutting lines for the other side of the quilt top and the top and bottom at 1½" from the bottom of the garlands. The length of the 4 sides should be the same, and measure approximately 76½" (depending on how much quilting is in the quilt).

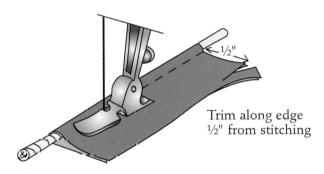

½"

Trim along edge ½" from stitching

FIG. 5–7. Making the piping using the zipper foot

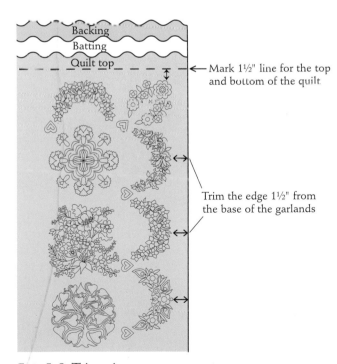

Backing
Batting
Quilt top

Mark 1½" line for the top and bottom of the quilt

Trim the edge 1½" from the base of the garlands

FIG. 5–8. Trimming measurements

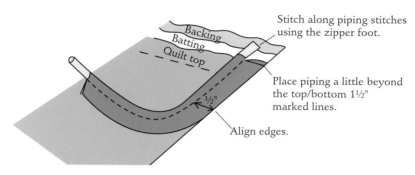

FIG. 5–9. Adding piping

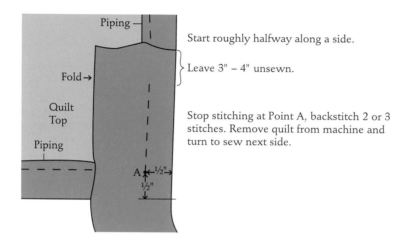

FIG. 5–10. Starting a mitered corner binding

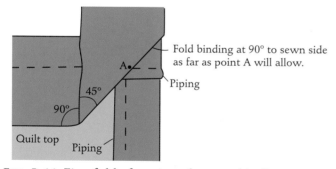

FIG. 5–11. First fold of a mitered corner binding

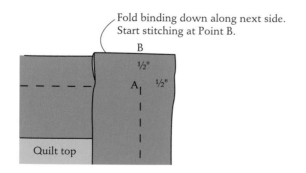

FIG. 5–12. Second fold of a mitered corner binding

Using the zipper foot, attach the piping to one side of the quilt, first checking that the piping overlaps the top and bottom edges' cutting lines before sewing it in place. Trim the other side of the quilt top and attach the piping (Fig. 5–9).

Trim across the top edge, trimming the piping ends at the same time. Attach the top piping. Trim across the bottom edge and attach the last strip of piping.

BINDING

Note that the binding for HEARTS AND GARLANDS finishes at ½" front and back.

Join the nine 3¼" x 40" strips to make the binding (see Fig. 5–6 on page 39). Press the binding strip in half all the way along its length, right-side out.

For binding with mitered corners, start sewing the binding part way along one side, leaving about 4" unsewn. Turn corners as in Figs. 5–10 through 5–12. Join ends at 45 degrees. Turn the binding and hand stitch it in place on the back.

PART 6
Appliqué Patterns

APPLIQUÉ BLOCK LAYOUT DIAGRAM

Corner Roses	Multi Garland	Poppy Garland	Star Garland	Yellow Garland	Pink Garland	Bluebell Garland	Corner Roses
Corner and garland row repeated	1 **A** A1 Tudor Rose	**B** B1 Four Hearts	**C** C1 Wisteria	**D** D1 Spring	**E** E1 Carnations		*Corner and garland row repeated*
	2 A2 Spiral	B2 Iris	C2 Lilies	D2 Tulips	E2 Summer		
	3 A3 Blue Poppies	B3 Pink Wreath	C3 Willow	D3 Bluebells	E3 Heart Tree		
	4 A4 Rose Square	B4 Basket Bouquet	C4 Multi Flora	D4 Peach Blooms	E4 Rose Ring		
	5 A5 Americana	B5 Holly and Ivy	C5 Daises	D5 Cornflower Ring	E5 Stars		
	Corner and garland row repeated						

A-1 *Tudor Rose*
Enlarge appliqué pattern 200%

B-1 *Four Hearts*

Enlarge appliqué pattern 200%

C-1 *Wisteria*

Enlarge appliqué pattern 200%

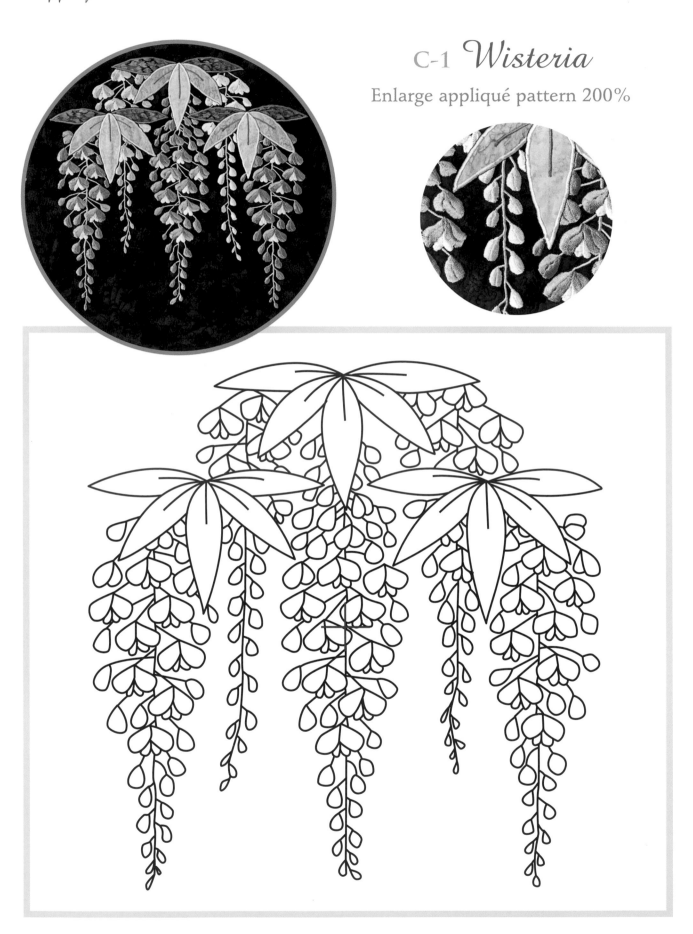

D-1 *Spring*

Enlarge appliqué pattern 200%

E-1 *Carnations*

Enlarge appliqué pattern 200%

A-2 *Spiral*

Enlarge appliqué pattern 200%

B-2 *Iris* (A)

Enlarge appliqué pattern 200%

B-2 *Iris* (B)

Enlarge appliqué pattern 200%

C-2 *Lilies*

Enlarge appliqué pattern 200%

D-2 *Tulips*

Enlarge appliqué pattern 200%

E-2 *Summer*

Enlarge appliqué pattern 200%

A-3 *Blue Poppies*

Enlarge appliqué pattern 200%

B-3 *Pink Wreath*

Enlarge appliqué pattern 200%

C-3 *Willow*

Enlarge appliqué pattern 200%

D-3 *Bluebells*

Enlarge appliqué pattern 200%

E-3 *Heart Tree*

Enlarge appliqué pattern 200%

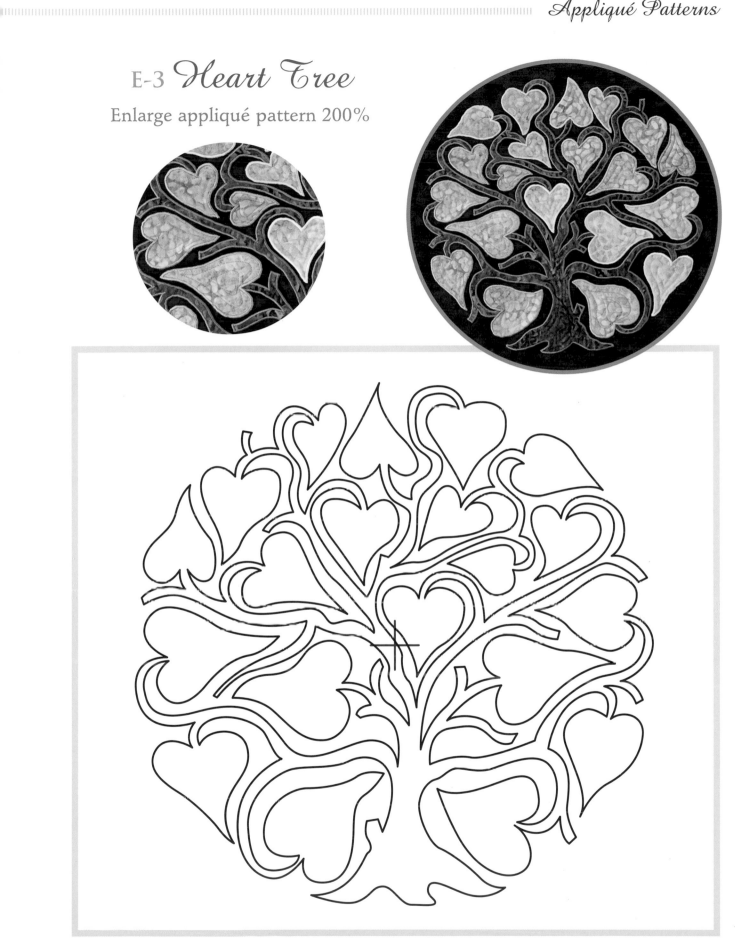

A-4 *Rose Square*

Enlarge appliqué pattern 200%

B-4 *Basket Bouquet*

Enlarge appliqué pattern 200%

C-4 *Multi Flora*

Enlarge appliqué pattern 200%

D-4 *Peach Blooms*

Enlarge appliqué pattern 200%

E-4 *Rose Ring*

Enlarge appliqué pattern 200%

A-5 *Americana*

Enlarge appliqué pattern 200%

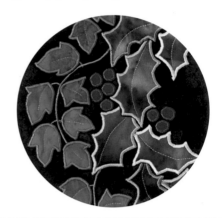

B-5 *Holly and Ivy*
Enlarge appliqué pattern 200%

C-5 *Daisies*

Enlarge appliqué pattern 200%

D-5 *Cornflower Ring*

Enlarge appliqué pattern 200%

E-5 *Stars*

Enlarge appliqué pattern 200%

Corner Roses

Appliqué pattern shown 100%

Multi Garland

Appliqué pattern
shown 100%

Poppy Garland

Appliqué pattern shown 100%

Star Garland

Appliqué pattern
shown 100%

Yellow Garland

Appliqué pattern shown 100%

Pink Garland

Appliqué pattern
shown 100%

Bluebell Garland

Appliqué pattern 100%

PART 7

Quilting Patterns

Refer to page 38, Fig. 5–4, key to quilting design placement.

Pattern 41

Pattern shown 100%
Trace 24

Pattern 42

Pattern shown 100%
Trace 28

Pattern 1

Enlarge quilting
patterns 200%

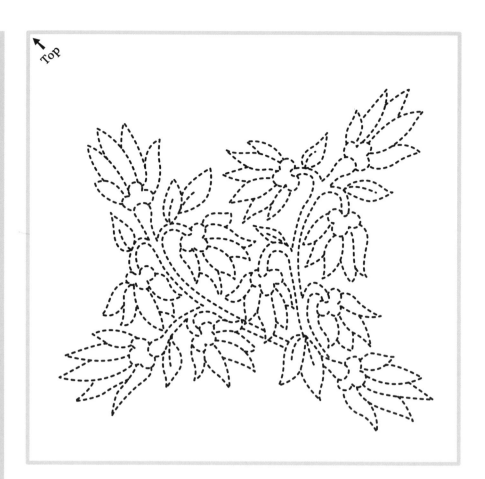

Pattern 2

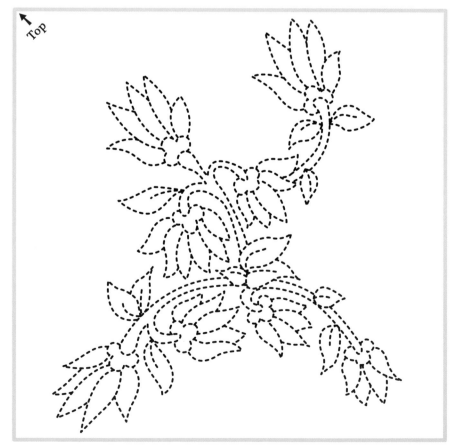

Flowers, Hearts & GARLANDS QUILT ❀ LIZ JONES

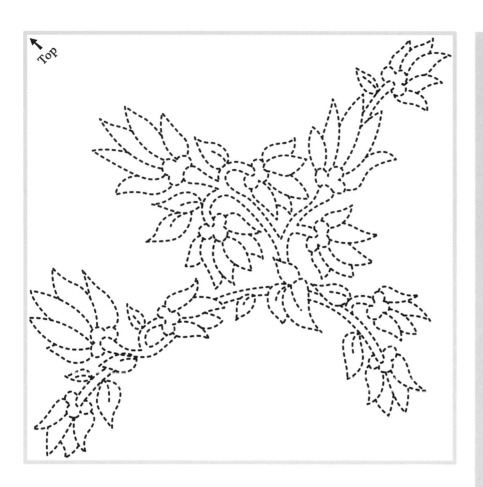

Pattern 4

Pattern 5

Enlarge quilting patterns 200%

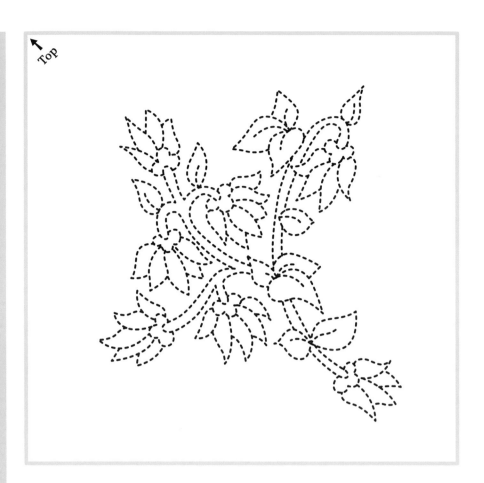

Pattern 6

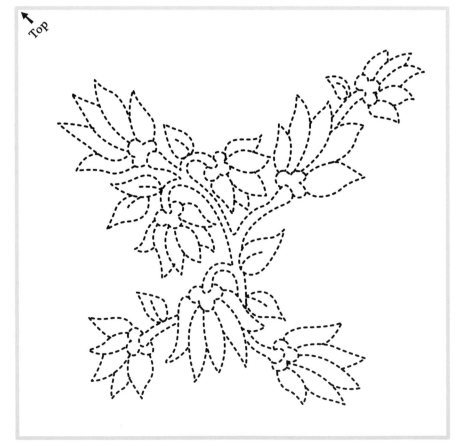

Pattern 7

Enlarge quilting
patterns 200%

Pattern 8

Pattern 9

Enlarge quilting
patterns 200%

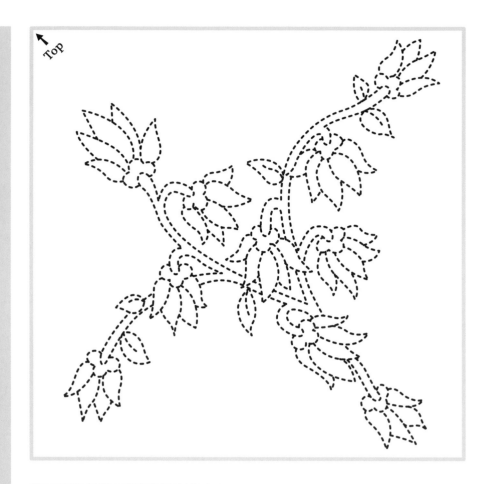

Pattern 10

Flowers, Hearts & GARLANDS QUILT ❀ LIZ JONES

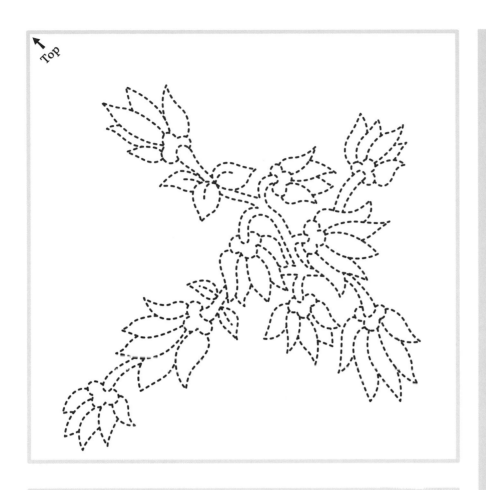

Enlarge quilting
patterns 200%

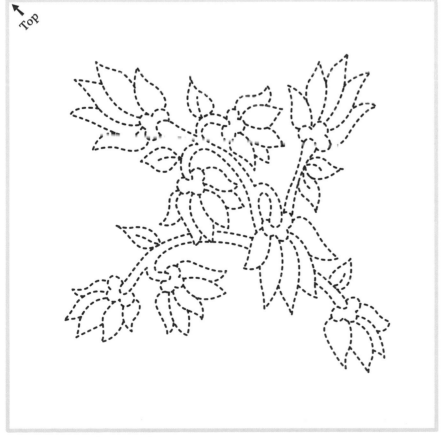

Pattern 12

Pattern 13

Enlarge quilting
patterns 200%

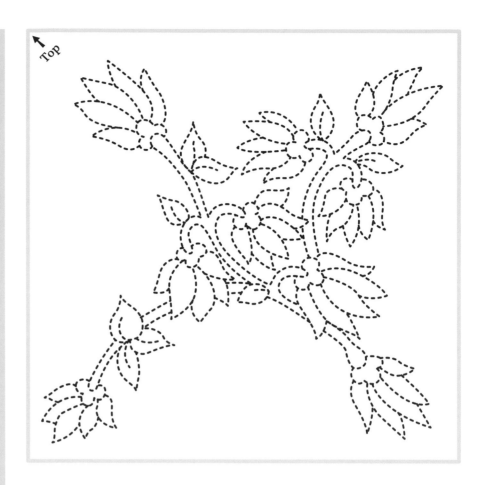

Pattern 14

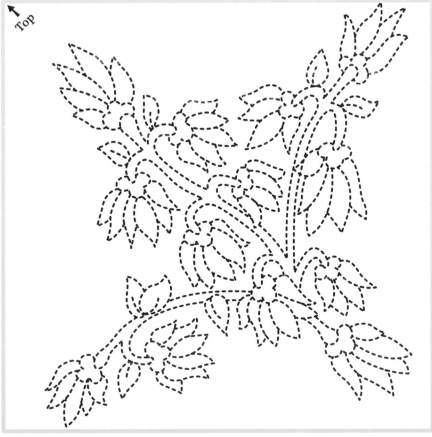

Pattern 16

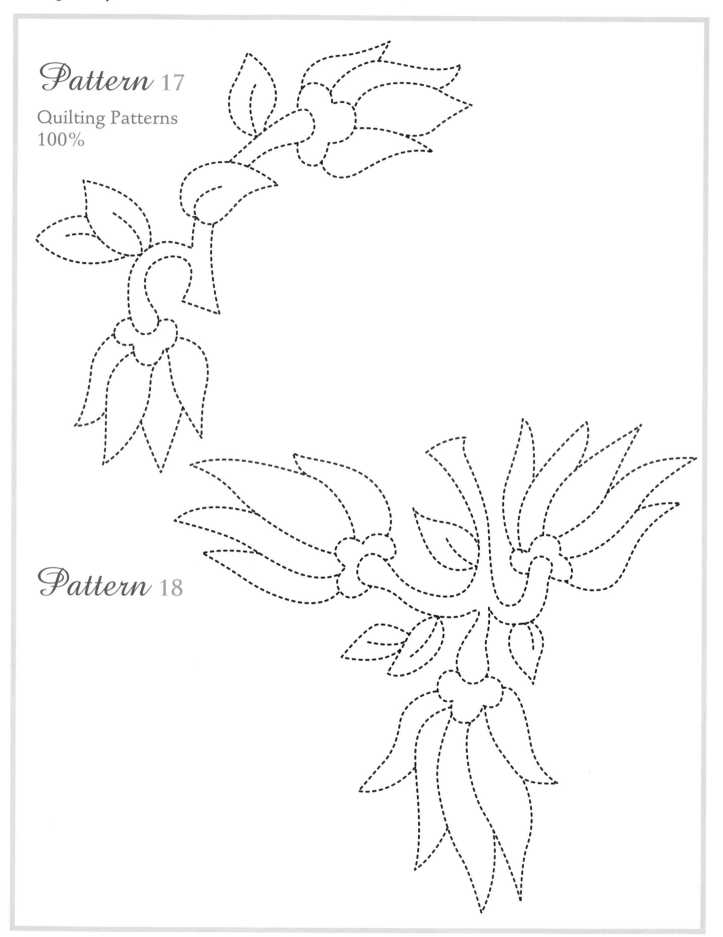

Pattern 17
Quilting Patterns
100%

Pattern 18

Pattern 19

Quilting Patterns
100%

Pattern 20

Pattern 21

Quilting Patterns
100%

Pattern 22

Pattern 23

Quilting Patterns
100%

Pattern 24

Pattern 25

Quilting Patterns 100%

Pattern 26

Pattern 27

Quilting Patterns
100%

Pattern 28

Pattern 29

Quilting Patterns 100%

Pattern 30

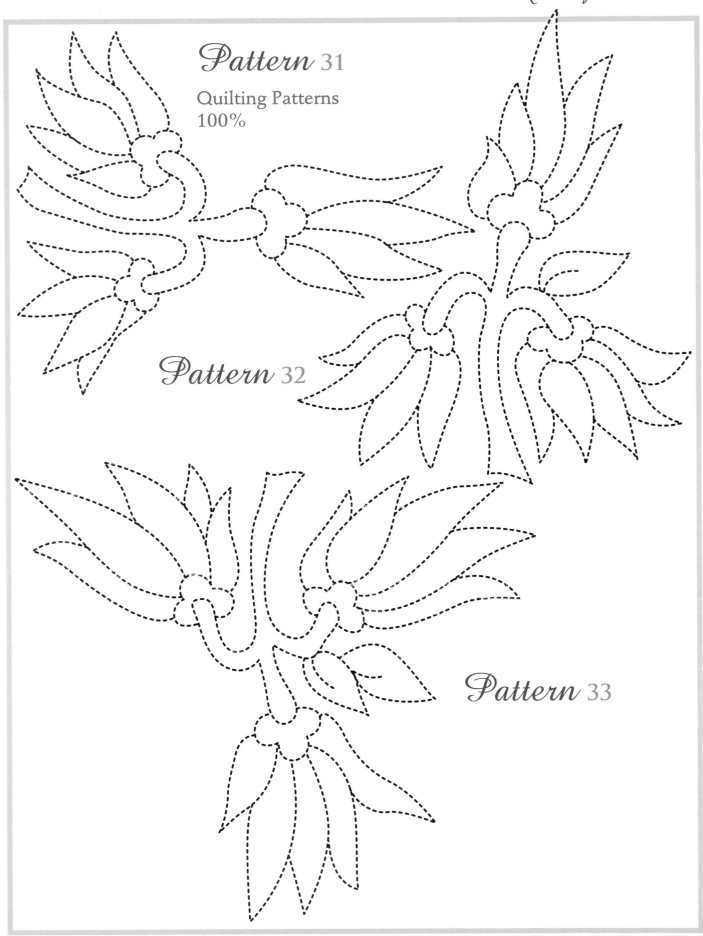

Pattern 31

Quilting Patterns
100%

Pattern 32

Pattern 33

Pattern 34

Quilting Patterns
100%

Pattern 35

Pattern 36

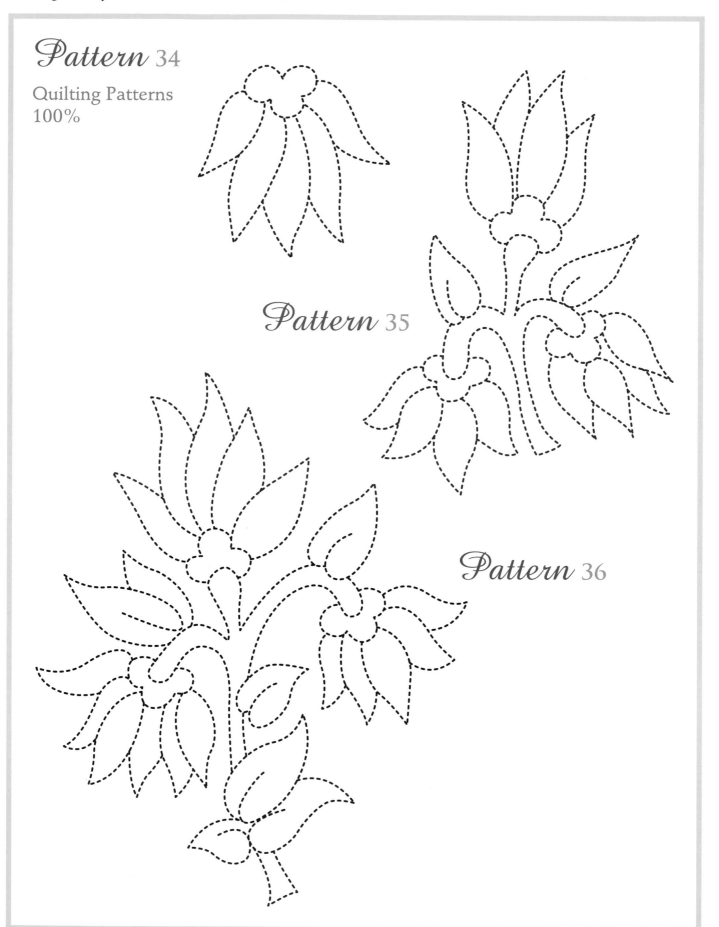

Pattern 37

Pattern 38

Quilting Patterns
100%

Pattern 40

Pattern 39

Bibliography

As there are so many beautiful and helpful books on quilting and associated techniques, I only mention the two to which I have turned most often over the years

Gaudynski, Diane. *Guide to Machine Quilting.* American Quilter's Society, 2002.

Pahl, Ellen. *The Quilter's Ultimate Visual Guide: From A to Z–Hundreds of Tips and Techniques for Successful Quiltmaking.* Rodale Press, Inc., 1997.

About the Author

Liz Jones has been interested in sewing most of her life. Her BA was in fine arts, followed by post-graduate studies in art history, and a teaching diploma. Her paints are now fabrics, and her canvases are quilts.

For most of the 1990s Liz worked in the former Yugoslavia—three years in Croatia with the United Nations and three years with the OSCE (Organization for Security and Cooperation in Europe) in Sarajevo. She discovered quilting in a magazine when passing through the Vienna airport in 1998—a life-changing moment!

She and her husband are avid travelers, and much of her inspiration is gleaned from plants and designs from all over the world with photography an important recording tool. Historical textiles are also a great source of inspiration. Her other passion is choral singing.

Liz's quilts have won numerous awards both in the United Kingdom and America, including the Pfaff Award for Machine Artistry (TUDOR ROSE), Houston 2004; and the Best of World 2008 (HEARTS AND GARLANDS) and Best of Country 2009 (SUMMER RISING) awards in the Mancuso World Quilt and Textile Shows. HEARTS AND GARLANDS also won the World of Beauty Award, Houston 2009, and was the logo quilt for the International Quilt Festival, Chicago 2010.

Flowers, Hearts & Garlands Quilt is her second book. As Liz Blacker, she wrote *Bromsgrove School Memorial Chapel Tapestries*, copyright Bromsgrove School 1993, a description of the 14 appliquéd wallhangings designed and made by her for Bromsgrove School, Worcestershire, U.K.

OTHER AQS BOOKS

This is only a small selection of the books available from the American Quilter's Society. AQS books are known worldwide for timely topics, clear writing, beautiful color photos, and accurate illustrations and patterns. The following books are available from your local bookseller, quilt shop, or public library.

#8351   US $26.95

#8151   US $24.95

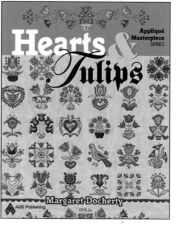

#7921   US $28.95

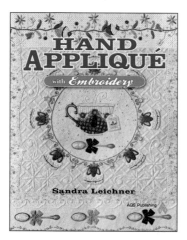

#8244   US $26.95

#8148   US $22.95

#7778   US $26.95

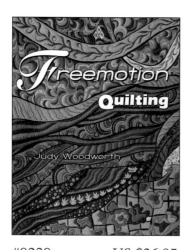

#8238   US $26.95

#8031   US $24.95

#8240   US $26.95